W9-CHK-845

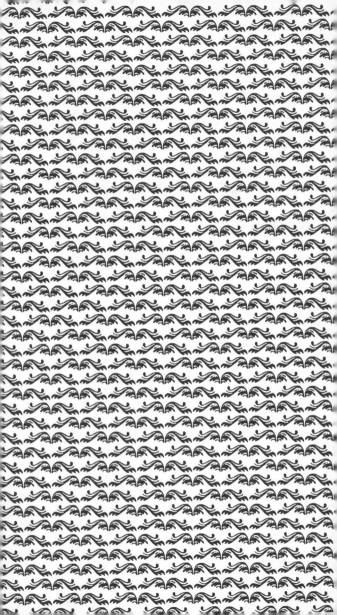

BENJAMIN FRANKLIN'S
BOOK OF VIRTUES

BENJAMIN FRANKLIN'S

Book of
VIRTUES

Applewood Books
Carlisle, Massachusetts

978-1-4290-9355-2

Copyright © 2016 Applewood Books, Inc.

"Portrait of Benjamin Franklin," engraving
by Henry Bryan Hall Sr., from the original portrait
painted from life by J. A. Duplessis in 1783.

10 9 8 7

MANUFACTURED IN THE UNITED STATES OF AMERICA
WITH AMERICAN-MADE MATERIALS

As I KNEW, or thought I knew, what was right and wrong, I did not see why I might not always do the one and avoid the other. But I soon found I had undertaken a task of more difficulty than I had imagined. While my care was employ'd in guarding against one fault, I was often surprised by another; habit took the advantage of inattention; inclination was sometimes too strong for reason. I concluded, at length, that the mere speculative conviction that it was our interest to be completely virtuous, was not sufficient to prevent our slipping; and that the contrary habits must be broken, and good ones acquired and established, before we can have any dependence on a steady, uniform rectitude of conduct. For this purpose I therefore contrived the following method.

IN THE VARIOUS ENUMERATIONS of the moral virtues I had met with in my reading, I found the catalogue more or less numerous, as different writers included more or fewer ideas under the same name. Temperance, for example, was by some confined to eating and drinking, while by others it was extended to mean the moderating of every other pleasure, appetite, inclination, or passion, bodily or mental, even to our avarice and ambition. I propos'd to myself, for the sake of clearness, to use rather more names, with fewer ideas annex'd to each, than a few names with more ideas; and I included under thirteen names of virtues all that at that time occurr'd to me as necessary or desirable, and annexed to each a short precept, which fully express'd the extent I gave to its meaning.

THESE NAMES OF VIRTUES, with their precepts, were:

1. TEMPERANCE. *Eat not to dullness; drink not to elevation.*

2. SILENCE. *Speak not but what may benefit others or yourself; avoid trifling conversation.*

3. ORDER. *Let all your things have their places; let each part of your business have its time.*

4. RESOLUTION. *Resolve to perform what you ought; perform without fail what you resolve.*

5. FRUGALITY. *Make no expense but to do good to others or yourself; i.e., waste nothing.*

6. INDUSTRY. *Lose no time; be always employ'd in something useful; cut off all unnecessary actions.*

7. SINCERITY. *Use no hurtful deceit; think innocently and justly, and, if you speak, speak accordingly.*

8. JUSTICE. *Wrong none by doing injuries, or omitting the benefits that are your duty.*

9. MODERATION. *Avoid extremes; forbear resenting injuries so much as you think they deserve.*

10. CLEANLINESS. *Tolerate no uncleanliness in body, clothes, or habitation.*

11. TRANQUILLITY. *Be not disturbed at trifles, or at accidents common or unavoidable.*

12. CHASTITY. *Rarely use venery but for health or offspring, never to dullness, weakness, or the injury of your own or another's peace or reputation.*

13. HUMILITY. *Imitate Jesus and Socrates.*

M Y INTENTION BEING to acquire the habitude of all these virtues, I judg'd it would be well not to distract my attention by attempting the whole at once, but to fix it on one of them at a time; and, when I should be master of that, then to proceed to another, and so on, till I should have gone thro' the thirteen; and, as the previous acquisition of some might facilitate the acquisition of certain others, I arrang'd them with that view, as they stand above. Temperance first, as it tends to procure that coolness and clearness of head, which is so necessary where constant vigilance was to be kept up, and guard maintained against the unremitting attraction of ancient habits, and the force of perpetual temptations. This being acquir'd and establish'd, Silence would be more easy; and my desire being to gain knowledge at the same time that I improv'd in virtue, and considering that in conversation it was obtain'd rather by the use of the ears than of the tongue, and therefore wishing to break a habit I was getting into of prattling, punning, and joking, which only made me acceptable to trifling company, I gave Silence the second place. This and the next, Order, I expected would allow me more time for attending to my project and my studies. Resolution, once become habitual, would keep me firm in my endeavors to obtain all the subsequent virtues; Frugality and Industry freeing me from my remaining debt, and producing affluence and independence, would make more easy the practice of Sincerity and Justice, etc., etc. Conceiving then, that, agreeably to the advice of Pythagoras in his Golden Verses, daily examination would be necessary, I contrived the following method for conducting that examination.

I MADE A LITTLE BOOK, in which I allotted a page for each of the virtues. I rul'd each page with red ink, so as to have seven columns, one for each day of the week, marking each column with a letter for the day. I cross'd these columns with thirteen red lines, marking the beginning of each line with the first letter of one of the virtues, on which line, and in its proper column, I might mark, by a little black spot, every fault I found upon examination to have been committed respecting that virtue upon that day.

Examination of Virtues

Eat not to dullness;
Drink not to elevation.

	Sun.	M.	T.	W.	Th.	F.	S.
Tem.							
Sil.							
Ord.							
Res.							
Fru.							
Ind.							
Sinc.							
Jus.							
Mod.							
Clea.							
Tran.							
Chas.							
Hum.							

✪ *To chart a year's progress go to bookofvirtues.awb.com.*

I DETERMINED to give a week's strict attention to each of the virtues successively. Thus, in the first week, my great guard was to avoid every the least offense against Temperance, leaving the other virtues to their ordinary chance, only marking every evening the faults of the day. Thus, if in the first week I could keep my first line, marked T, clear of spots, I suppos'd the habit of that virtue so much strengthen'd and its opposite weaken'd, that I might venture extending my attention to include the next, and for the following week keep both lines clear of spots. Proceeding thus to the last, I could go thro' a course complete in thirteen weeks, and four courses in a year. And like him who, having a garden to weed, does not attempt to eradicate all the bad herbs at once, which would exceed his reach and his strength, but works on one of the beds at a time, and, having accomplish'd the first, proceeds to a second, so I should have, I hoped, the encouraging pleasure of seeing on my pages the progress I made in virtue, by clearing successively my lines of their spots, till in the end, by a number of courses, I should be happy in viewing a clean book, after a thirteen weeks' daily examination.

THIS MY LITTLE BOOK had for its motto these lines from Addison's *Cato*:

Here will I hold. If there's a power above us
(And that there is all nature cries aloud
Thro' all her works), He must delight in virtue;
And that which he delights in must be happy.

Another from Cicero:

O vitae Philosophia dux! O virtutum indaga-
trixexpultrixque vitiorum! Unus dies, bene et
ex praeceptis tuis actus, peccanti immortalitati
est anteponendus.

Another from the Proverbs of Solomon, speaking of wisdom or virtue:

Length of days is in her right hand, and in
her left hand riches and honour. Her ways
are ways of pleasantness, and all her paths
are peace.   —III. 16, 17.

And conceiving God to be the fountain of
wisdom, I thought it right and necessary
to solicit his assistance for obtaining it; to
this end I formed the following little prayer,
which was prefix'd to my tables of examination, for daily use.

O powerful Goodness! bountiful Father!
merciful Guide! increase in me that wisdom
which discovers my truest interest! Strengthen
my resolutions to perform what that wisdom
dictates. Accept my kind offices to thy other
children as the only return in my power for
thy continual favors to me.

I used also sometimes a little prayer, which I
took from Thomson's poems, viz.:

Father of light and life, thou Good Supreme!
O teach me what is good; teach me Thyself!
Save me from folly, vanity, and vice,
From every low pursuit; and fill my soul
With knowledge, conscious peace, and virtue
pure; Sacred, substantial, never-fading bliss!

THE PRECEPT OF ORDER requiring that every part of my business should have its allotted time, one page in my little book contain'd the following scheme of employment for the twenty-four hours of a natural day:

THE MORNING.

5 AM: *Rise, wash, & address.*

QUESTION. What good shall I do this day?

6 AM: *Powerful Goodness! Contrive day's business, and take the resolution of the day.*

7 AM: *Prosecute the present study, & breakfast.*

9 AM: *Work.*

NOON: *Read, or overlook my accounts, & dine.*

3 PM: *Work.*

EVENING.

6 PM: *Put things in their places.*

7 PM: *Supper. Music or diversion, or conversation.*

QUESTION. What good have I done today?

8 PM: *Examination of the day.*

NIGHT.

I AM: *Sleep.*

I ENTER'D UPON THE EXECUTION of this plan for self-examination, and continu'd it with occasional intermissions for some time. I was surpris'd to find myself so much fuller of faults than I had imagined; but I had the satisfaction of seeing them diminish. To avoid the trouble of renewing now and then my little book, which, by scraping out the marks on the paper of old faults to make room for new ones in a new course, became full of holes, I transferr'd my tables and precepts to the ivory leaves of a memorandum book, on which the lines were drawn with red ink, that made a durable stain, and on those lines I mark'd my faults with a black-lead pencil, which marks I could easily wipe out with a wet sponge. After a while I went thro' one course only in a year, and afterward only one in several years, till at length I omitted them entirely, being employ'd in voyages and business abroad, with a multiplicity of affairs that interfered; but I always carried my little book with me.

MY SCHEME OF ORDER gave me the most trouble; and I found that, tho' it might be practicable where a man's business was such as to leave him the disposition of his time, that of a journeyman printer, for instance, it was not possible to be exactly observed by a master, who must mix with the world, and often receive people of business at their own hours. Order, too, with regard to places for things, papers, etc., I found extremely difficult to acquire. I had not been early accustomed to it, and, having an exceeding good memory, I was not so sensible of the inconvenience attending want of method.

I was surpris'd to find myself so much fuller of faults than I had imagined.

Order, too, with regard to places for things, papers, etc., I found extremely difficult to acquire.

This article, therefore, cost me so much painful attention, and my faults in it vexed me so much, and I made so little progress in amendment, and had such frequent relapses, that I was almost ready to give up the attempt, and content myself with a faulty character in that respect, like the man who, in buying an ax of a smith, my neighbour, desired to have the whole of its surface as bright as the edge. The smith consented to grind it bright for him if he would turn the wheel; he turn'd, while the smith press'd the broad face of the ax hard and heavily on the stone, which made the turning of it very fatiguing. The man came every now and then from the wheel to see how the work went on, and at length would take his ax as it was, without farther grinding. "No," said the smith, "turn on, turn on; we shall have it bright by-and-by; as yet, it is only speckled." "Yes," said the man, "but I think I like a speckled ax best." And I believe this may have been the case with many, who, having, for want of some such means as I employ'd, found the difficulty of obtaining good and breaking bad habits in other points of vice and virtue, have given up the struggle, and concluded that "a speckled ax was best"; for something, that pretended to be reason, was every now and then suggesting to me that such extreme nicety as I exacted of would make me ridiculous; that a perfect character might be attended with the

A perfect character might be attended with the inconvenience of being envied and hated; and that a benevolent man should allow a few faults in himself, to keep his friends in countenance.

inconvenience of being envied and hated; and that a benevolent man should allow a few faults in himself, to keep his friends in countenance.

IN TRUTH, I found myself incorrigible with respect to Order; and now I am grown old, and my memory bad, I feel very sensibly the want of it. But, on the whole, tho' I never arrived at the perfection I had been so ambitious of obtaining, but fell far short of it, yet I was, by the endeavor, a better and a happier man than I otherwise should have been if I had not attempted it; as those who aim at perfect writing by imitating the engraved copies, tho' they never reach the wish'd-for excellence of those copies, their

As those who aim at perfect writing by imitating the engraved copies, tho' they never reach the wish'd-for excellence of those copies, their hand is mended by the endeavor, and is tolerable while it continues fair and legible.

hand is mended by the endeavor, and is tolerable while it continues fair and legible.

IT MAY BE WELL my posterity should be informed that to this little artifice, with the blessing of God, their ancestor ow'd the constant felicity of his life, down to his 79th year, in which this is written. What reverses may attend the remainder is in the hand of Providence; but, if they arrive, the reflection on past happiness enjoy'd ought to help his bearing them with more resignation. To Temperance he ascribes his long-continued health, and what is still left to him of a good constitution; to Industry and Frugality, the early easiness of his circumstances and acquisition of his fortune, with all

I was, by the endeavor, a better and a happier man than I otherwise should have been if I had not attempted it.

that knowledge that enabled him to be a useful citizen, and obtained for him some degree of reputation among the learned; to Sincerity and Justice, the confidence of his country, and the honorable employs it conferred upon him; and to the joint influence of the whole mass of the virtues, even in the imperfect state he was able to acquire them, all that evenness of temper, and that cheerfulness in conversation, which makes his company still sought for, and agreeable even to his younger acquaintance. I hope, therefore, that some of my descendants may follow the example and reap the benefit.

I T WILL BE REMARK'D that, tho' my scheme was not wholly without religion, there was in it no mark of any of the distinguishing tenets of any particular sect. I had purposely avoided them; for, being fully persuaded of the utility and excellency of my method, and that it might be serviceable to people in all religions, and intending some time or other to publish it, I would not have any thing in it that should prejudice any one, of any sect, against it. I purposed writing a little comment on each virtue, in which I would have shown the advantages of possessing it, and the mischiefs attending its opposite vice; and I should have called my book *The Art of Virtue*, because it would have shown the means and manner of obtaining virtue, which would have distinguished it from the mere exhortation to be good, that does not instruct and indicate

I hope, therefore, that some of my descendants may follow the example and reap the benefit.

the means, but is like the apostle's man of verbal charity, who "only without showing to the naked and hungry how or where they might get clothes or victuals, exhorted them to be fed and clothed" (JAMES II. 15,16).

BUT IT SO HAPPENED that my intention of writing and publishing this comment was never fulfilled. I did, indeed, from time to time, put down short hints of the sentiments, reasonings, etc., to be made use of in it, some of which I have still by me; but the necessary close attention to private business in the earlier part of my life, and public business since, have occasioned my postponing it; for, it being connected in my mind with a great and extensive project, that required the whole man to execute, and which an unforeseen succession of employs prevented my attending to, it has hitherto remain'd unfinish'd.

IN THIS PIECE it was my design to explain and enforce this doctrine, that vicious actions are not hurtful because they are forbidden, but forbidden because they are hurtful, the nature of man alone considered; that it was, therefore, every one's interest to be virtuous who wish'd to be happy even in this world; and I should, from this circumstance (there being always in the world a number of rich merchants, nobility, states, and princes, who have need of honest instruments for the management of their affairs, and such being so rare), have endeavored to

Vicious actions are not hurtful because they are forbidden, but forbidden because they are hurtful.

convince young persons that no qualities were so likely to make a poor man's fortune as those of probity and integrity.

MY LIST OF VIRTUES contain'd at first but twelve; but a Quaker friend having kindly informed me that I was generally thought proud; that my pride show'd itself frequently in conversation; that I was not content with being in the right when discussing any point, but was overbearing, and rather insolent, of which he convinc'd me by mentioning several instances; I determined endeavoring to cure myself, if I could, of this vice or folly among the rest, and I added Humility to my list, giving an extensive meaning to the word.

I CANNOT BOAST of much success in acquiring the reality of this virtue, but I had a good deal with regard to the appearance of it. I made it a rule to forbear all direct contradiction to the sentiments of others, and all positive assertion of my own. I even forbid myself, agreeably to the old laws of our Junto, the use of every word or expression in the language that imported a fix'd opinion, such as certainly, undoubtedly, etc., and I adopted, instead of them, I conceive, I apprehend, or I imagine a thing to be so or so; or it so appears to me at present. When another asserted something that I thought an error, I deny'd myself the pleasure of contradicting him abruptly, and of showing immedi-

I soon found the advantage of this change in my manner; the conversations I engag'd in went on more pleasantly.

25

The modest way in which I propos'd my opinions procur'd them a readier reception and less contradiction.

ately some absurdity in his proposition; and in answering I began by observing that in certain cases or circumstances his opinion would be right, but in the present case there appear'd or seem'd to me some difference, etc. I soon found the advantage of this change in my manner; the conversations I engag'd in went on more pleasantly. The modest way in which I propos'd my opinions procur'd them a readier reception and less contradiction; I had less mortification when I was found to be in the wrong, and I more easily prevail'd with others to give up their mistakes and join with me when I happened to be in the right.

AND THIS MODE, which I at first put on with some violence to natural inclination, became at length so easy, and so habitual to me, that perhaps for these fifty years past no one has ever heard a dogmatical expression escape me. And to this habit (after my character of integrity) I think it principally owing that I had early so much weight with my fellow-citizens when I proposed new institutions, or alterations in the old, and so much influence in public councils when I became a member; for I was but a bad speaker, never eloquent, subject to much hesitation in my choice of words, hardly correct in language, and yet I generally carried my points.

IN REALITY, there is, perhaps, no one of our natural passions so hard to subdue as pride. Disguise it, struggle with it, beat it down, stifle it, mortify it as much as one pleases, it is still alive, and will every now and then peep out and show itself; you will see it, perhaps, often in this history; for, even if I could conceive that I had completely overcome it, I should probably be proud of my humility.

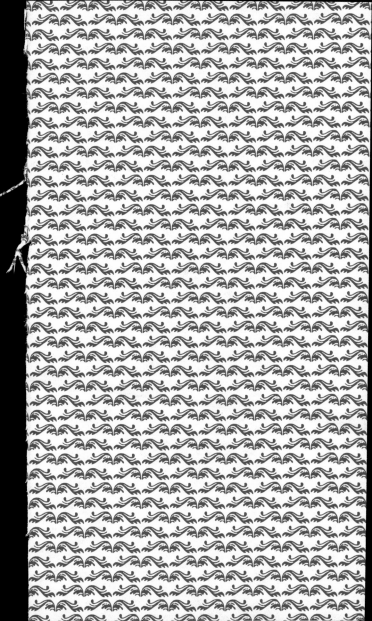

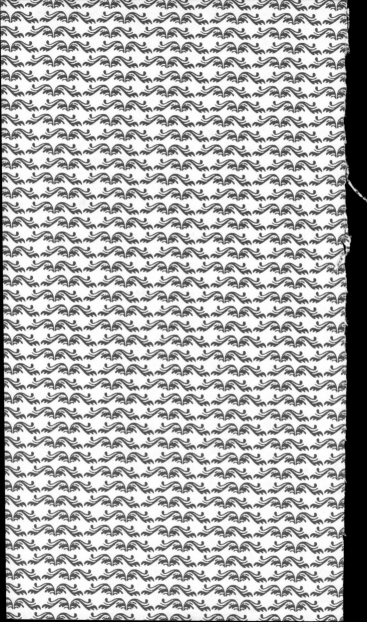